HORSES WERE BORN
TO BE ON GRASS

*How We Discovered the Simple but Undeniable
Truth About Grass, Sugar, Equine
Diet, and Lifestyle*

Copyright © 2011 by Joe Camp

Photos © 2011 by Kathleen Camp

All rights reserved.

Published in the United States by 14 Hands Press,

an imprint of Camp Horse Camp, LLC

www.14handspress.com

Library of Congress subject headings

Camp, Joe

Horses Were Born to be On Grass / by Joe Camp

Horses

Human-animal relationships

Horses-health

Horsemanship

The Soul of a Horse: Life Lessons from the Herd

ISBN 978-1-930681-39-2

First Edition

HORSES WERE BORN
TO BE ON GRASS

*How We Discovered the Simple but Undeniable
Truth About Grass, Sugar, Equine
Diet, and Lifestyle*

JOE CAMP

14 HANDS PRESS

Also by Joe Camp

The National Best Seller
The Soul of a Horse
Life Lessons from the Herd

The Highly Acclaimed Best Selling Sequel
Born Wild
The Soul of a Horse

Horses & Stress
Eliminating the Root Cause of Most Health, Hoof & Behavior Problems

Why Relationship First Works
Why and How It Changes Everything

Beginning Ground Work
Everything We've Learned About Relationship and Leadership

Training with Treats
*With Relationship and Basic Training Locked In Treats Can Be
an Excellent Way to Enhance Good Communication*

God Only Knows
Can You Trust Him with the Secret?

Why Our Horses Are Barefoot
*Everything We've Learned About the
Health and Happiness of the Hoof*

The Soul of a Horse Blogged
The Journey Continues

Horses Without Grass
*How We Kept Six Horses Moving and Eating Happily
Healthily on an Acre and a Half of Rocks and Dirt*

Who Needs Hollywood
The Amazing Story of How Benji Became the #3 Movie of the Year

Dog On It
Everything You Need To Know About Life Is Right There At Your Feet

"Joe Camp is a master storyteller." - *THE NEW YORK TIMES*

"Joe Camp is a natural when it comes to understanding how animals tick and a genius at telling us their story. His books are must-reads for those who love animals of any species." - *MONTY ROBERTS, AUTHOR OF NEW YORK TIMES BEST-SELLER THE MAN WHO LISTENS TO HORSES*

"The tightly written, simply designed, and powerfully drawn chapters often read like short stories that flow from the heart. Camp has become something of a master at telling us what can be learned from animals, in this case specifically horses, without making us realize we have been educated, and, that is, perhaps, the mark of a real teacher." - *JACK L. KENNEDY, THE JOPLIN INDEPENDENT*

"One cannot help but be touched by Camp's love and sympathy for animals and by his eloquence on the subject." - *MICHAEL KORDA, THE WASHINGTON POST*

"Joe Camp is a gifted storyteller and the results are magical. Joe entertains, educates and empowers, baring his own soul while articulating keystone principles of a modern revolution in horsemanship." - *RICK LAMB, AUTHOR AND TV/RADIO HOST "THE HORSE SHOW"*

For Kathleen, who loved me enough to initiate all this
when she was secretly terrified of horses

CONTENTS

INTRODUCTION

Often, in the early evening, when the stresses of the day are weighing heavy, I pack it in and head out to the pasture. I'll sit on my favorite rock, or just stand, with my shoulders slumped, head down, and wait. It's never long before I feel the magical tickle of whiskers against my neck, or the elixir of warm breath across my ear, a restoring rub against my cheek. I have spoken their language and they have responded. And my problems have vanished. This book is written for everyone who has never experienced this miracle.

- Joe Camp
The Soul of a Horse
Life Lessons from the Herd

1
FOUNDER VALLEY

Horses were born to be on grass. We know this from their 52 million-year evolution out in the Great Plains and Great Basin of the western United States. All of which was without any help from us humans.

So why were we being told that our horses couldn't be out on grass 24/7 when we moved from southern California to middle Tennessee? It didn't make any sense. What was I missing? One of the reasons we were making the move was to finally be able to let our horses live like horses.

This was all getting very scary.

The morning we fed our herd for the last time on their dusty rocky hillside in southern California Kathleen and I had to work at holding ourselves together. The gang seemed to know something was afoot, especially when I walked out of the gate with all five of their tubs. We realized that we had never recorded the entire procedure before and this would be the last opportunity so Kathleen had the video camera rolling. Seemed appropriate somehow that we were documenting the final California feed. (See the Video: *Our California Paddock Paradise. What We Did. How We Did It. And Why* on Vimeo & The Soul of a Horse Channel on YouTube)

Only now was it occurring to me that we were actually going to do this. The horse transport was coming later that afternoon. The first set of movers the next day. The tractor and the Gator were leaving the following day. That night was the world premiere of my youngest son's directing debut (*Love Happens*). The following morning Kathleen, Benji and I were to climb on a plane and fly into Nashville, and the next day the horses would arrive in Bell Buckle. Being so wrapped up in the details of the process had helped me push aside how scary it all really was. But now it was here. We were about to tell our horses goodbye and send them off on the road.

It took over six months of searching, planning, and execution to bring all this together but it seemed like it happened overnight. Like one of those impulsive decisions made in an instant that brings on the shivers. That, we discovered, is what our big new front porch overlooking the pasture was for.

Shiver removal.

Our timing was perfect. The move landed us right in the middle of record-setting rainfall in Tennessee. Seven inches the day the horses came in. And it rained for days prior to their arrival. Gail Murphy's Personalized Equine Transportation Service has a reputation for never being late, but on this day they were. The rains slowed them to a crawl causing them to arrive after dark. Which is when we learned that the turn onto our road was too tight for their rig to make. We had to shuttle the horses off the transport trailer onto our 3-horse trailer which had to be pulled by a generous new neighbor with his 4-wheel drive tractor because my truck would've been mud-bound for sure.

Noelle, our new mustang, went into a paddock in front of the barn and the hillside herd of five got the paddock behind the barn for the night. We didn't think it wise to turn them out on a steep unfamiliar *muddy* hillside at night. *Is that another one of those human things like blankets in the snow :).* They hadn't been out of the trailer for ten minutes when every one of them began to wallow in the mud like little pigs.

And through it all I could only think about what all this wet and mud might do to their beautiful, dry, rock-solid barefoot hooves.

Everyone was in fine (but muddy) shape the next morning. Noelle, our mustang who had not been with the herd as yet, was thoroughly enjoying being just over the fence and everybody seemed quite relaxed for being in such a strange place after travelling more than 2000 miles across the country.

We checked the footing on the smaller of the two pastures, the one closest to the house, and decided to open the gate let 'em have at it. It was definitely a Yeee-Haaww moment. Cash, my co-author and cover boy on *The Soul of a Horse*, trotted through of the gate and without ever looking back broke into a full gallop up the steep hill and off toward the house. Within moments the other four were right behind him. Running, romping, and kicking up their heels! Kathleen got it all on video but no stills unfortunately. (*The video will someday make it to The Soul of a Horse YouTube Channel.*) It was something to see. Poor Noelle could only hang by the fence and pace. And bellow at them.

When the herd finally calmed down their joy escalated into disbelief. There was grass everywhere! I'm pretty sure that four of the five had lived their entire lives in the west and had never seen anything like this. They were fun to watch, but it was also more than a little bit scary. We had received numerous warnings that horses could not come here from the deserts of southern California and be out 24/7 on the very "rich grasses of

middle Tennessee." Too much sugar in this grass, we were told. Some had called the area "Founder Valley." I can tell you it's not easy sticking to your convictions when being peppered with epithets like *Founder Valley*. I was worried about it to be sure, but I had done enough study of horses in the wild to feel that something was amiss with the local logic. It's more complex than just sugar in grass. All grass everywhere in the world generates sugar. Could soil differences alone cause an over abundance? And how much does lots and lots of movement play into positive digestion and metabolism? Can supplements balance other things that if left unbalanced would be bad for the horse? And how much can stress from confinement and human-adjusted lifestyle play into metabolism imbalances. I didn't know, but I was already researching to find out. As mentioned, one of the points of moving here was to be able to truly let the horses live like horses. Like they were genetically designed to live. And I wouldn't give that up without knowledge certain.

I was reminded of a piece I had read in a book about the San Diego Zoo's adoption of two gorillas they wanted to mate. They fed the exact same leaves the gorillas had been eating in the wild, or so they thought. But the gorillas did not do well and did not mate. After a bunch of further research they finally discovered that when they were washing the leaves (so they'd be nice and clean) they were removing all the little bugs and microscopic life that were actually adding 10% to 15% animal protein to the gorilla diets. They quit washing the leaves and the gorillas got better immediately, and mated.

So I was on a mission to "find the bugs" so to speak. To discover why horses in the wild can spend their entire spring and summer on beautiful rich-looking meadows and do just fine, but horses (or at least *some* horses) in middle Tennessee can't. The answers I found made an interesting study into the way we humans think.

The first thing I discovered was that just when you think you have everything figured out God says, "Not so fast". We simply didn't count on moving into record rainfall. And tons of mud in the pre-selected morning and evening supplement feed zones. I'm glad the washer and dryer were immediately hooked up because I was sliding through a pair of muddy jeans a day! God just wanted us to know after so much complaining about the dust in California that the opposite of dust has its downside as well :).

All the horses learned right away that water was now from a pond instead of a big metal tub. Skeeter immediately got into the swing and went almost up to his knees. Even Cash who especially hates touching water with his feet drank his fill and it wasn't long before Mouse leapt in belly first.

2

FINDING THE BUGS
STEP ONE

It turned out to be the wettest fall on record in middle Tennessee. We had over 26 inches during our first six weeks.

I was worried about their feet in such squishy conditions but that worry was trumped by the rich grass warning. I had to solve that issue. I had to find those bugs. I had already learned that wild horses don't founder on grass. And some domestic horses do. And I was determined to find out why. Like the earlier story of the two gorillas at the San Diego Zoo, there had to be answers. And the logical place to begin is out there where there is no human intervention. Where no one is washing the bugs off the leaves. Out there in the wild.

During our first tele-workshop on *Why Barefoot?* we drifted into the role that diet and nutrition play in the barefoot lifestyle (huge!) and there was much talk about Spring grasses, high sugar content, etc. After the workshop I was glancing over some of the questions from participants, and Ginger Kathren's PBS series of "Cloud" documentaries that follow one particular wild herd in Montana's Pryor Mountains came to mind. Every Spring, once the snow has melted enough, the wild horses head for a beautiful huge meadow on top of the mountain, staying there for most of the Spring, Summer, and early Fall. So I asked Eddie Drabek (natural hoof specialist and one of our workshop hosts): "What's the difference? If Spring grasses are not supposed to be good for horses, then how do these mustangs get by. How do they deal with it. To our knowledge none of them have ever foundered because of the Spring/Summer grasses."

Eddie's answer was, I thought, brilliant. Loaded with super information, analysis, and a road map of questions for further research. It follows. The underlines are mine.

Joe – In the wild the grasses are native grasses…and unstressed grasses. Of course I realize there are times of drought but typically grasses left in their natural state handle such things quite well because they are going through the natural cycle they are meant to go through. They're <u>never mown down</u> (other than naturally grazed, over time, each year), <u>never overwatered, with no pesticides or chemical fertilizer,</u> and not encouraged to grow in a season they aren't meant to. Also <u>the wild horse meadow is not just one kind of rich lush "genetically improved" grass,</u> like all Orchard, or what not. It's a mix. The horses have CHOICE. And the wild area is not lush and thick. Compared to many domestic pastures, wild meadow grasses are fairly scattered, which would help slow grazing and create more browsing…which helps the digestive system handle things more efficiently.

Some native species of grasses are rich, others are not. And these "non-rich" grasses with lower starches/sugars can cut or dilute the sugar of the richer grasses.

Every spring I see changes in my horses hooves…some rings, maybe they lose a little concavity here and there. Not enough to make them sore but I keep my two founder-prone ponies drylotted or they would show more damage. Why? <u>Because our grass pretty much stays stressed</u>. We have nothing but bright green little nubs of "candy grass" as I call it, since the pasture is overgrazed…I have too many horses on too small of acreage, so not much I can do other than keep them penned up the majority of the time which I hate doing of course.

I trim for a few clients who have large 40-50 acre pastures, with just 4-5 horses and tall healthy grass. A small few will show some minor changes but the majority have no problems at all. At least the ones not being fed sweet feed. That's because the grasses are healthy, and non-stressed, thus much lower in starch/sugar. And typically on larger acreage there are a lot of native grasses, not all one type as in small paddocks.

Mustangs start to drop weight in the fall typically, after getting a great weight during spring/summer. This

is as nature intended. They get lean after a hard winter
with less forage, and what forage is there is dry and
dormant. Then spring hits and the horses are more able
to handle spring grasses because they *need* it coming out
of winter. Many of the mares are in final stages of
pregnancy, they definitely need it to get ready for baby. If they started out being fat and chunky after winter
and were put on the spring grass this might be a much
different scenario.

Most domestic horses don't *need* the rich grasses to
"come out of winter" the way a wild horse does, which
is why it can cause them issues. We keep them fed and
fat through winter… and panic if they do drop some
weight. What's worse…we keep feeding them the same
exact amount of grain/feed, alfalfa, etc. we were feeding
through winter, PLUS now they are getting grass. I tell
people all the time, if they are getting a lot of grass,
you MUST cut back on everything else (really they
probably need *nothing* else). But people still
feed…asking them to quit feeding pellets or grain I've
found is like asking them to give away their first born
child. They look at you like you are plum crazy.

Also, there's movement in the wild. The mustangs are getting a lot of movement. A lot! This helps
so much; is *necessary*! They aren't being confined, they
have good firm ground. They aren't living on soft shav-
ings or arena sand part of their day, aren't getting
grains, sweet feeds, or alfalfa, etc.

And here's something most folks never think about: Domestic horses, <u>particularly those that are stalled during part of the night/day, tend to gorge when let out on pasture</u>, even when it's baking hot. Their inner clocks are amazing...they know when it's about time for them to be caught up and taken back to their pen or stall and they'll begin to "gorge" when they know that time is running out.

Nothing has changed more in natural hoof care than the diet info. The trim is the same, but diet thoughts change each week it seems. For instance now many are questioning Soy and this is what they hoped would be a safer alternative to alfala/corn based feeds. It is definitely something I wish more people would research...and quit researching in the labs of Purina and Nutrena, and research extensively in the wild habitats...what we could learn would be fantastic. – Eddie

3
FINDING THE BUGS
STEP TWO

As Spring began to flower in Tennessee and little green nubblets of grass began to come alive I was once again reminded by several people that our horses shouldn't be out 24/7 on the "rich grasses of middle Tennessee." These warnings ramped up my motivation to find answers to the puzzling question of why some domestic horses founder on grass. I was on a mission to prove or disprove Eddie's hypothesis.

First I reviewed my list of Undeniable Truths developed for our two tele-workshops on *Why Barefoot* and *Diet and Nutrition*. These are known and proven truths of science, not conjecture or opinion. The ones that apply to this issue are:

1. Science confirms that it would take a minimum of 5000 years – probably closer to 10,000 – to even begin to change the base genetics of *any* species. In other words, a few hundred years of selective breeding has no effect on base genetics whatsoever. Which means that the domestic horse and the horse in the wild are genetically exactly the same.

2. DNA sequencing was performed on bones of horses discovered in the Alaskan permafrost da-

ting 12,000 to 28,000 years old and the results were compared to DNA sequencing from today's domestic horse. There was less than 1.2% difference between the two. Again confirming that the genetics of every horse on the planet are the same, and that "every horse on the planet retains the ability to return successfully to the wild or feral state." Note the scientists use the word: *successfully.* In other words, today's domestic horse has the genetic ability to grow as perfect a foot and take care of himself with no help from humans every bit as well as those in the wild.

3. The horse evolved for more than 50 million years in the Great Basin of the western United States. During those millions of years he developed genetics designed to *survive* and live in a specific lifestyle in a specific manner. To eat in a specific way. To move a specific amount. To socialize in a way that provides for a specific need. The domestic horse of today retains those genetics which program his lifestyle to:

   a. Move a minimum of eight to twenty miles every day of his life in search of food, water, and staying ahead of predators. Living in a stall without this movement causes physical and mental stress to the horse.

   b. Eat tiny bits of forage – mostly *grass* forage - little bits at a time, virtually around the clock; a minimum of 16-18 hours a day, or more. Their tummies are tiny and not meant to eat two or three large meals a day, and their hindgut *requires* the constant passage of grass forage through it in order to perform and digest as designed. In other words, the horse needs *free choice* grass forage or grass hay 24/7.

c. Live within a herd. For safety, not for fun. There is safety in numbers. Separation from the herd creates emotional stress, and emotional stress attacks the physical body, and bad things happen.

d. Have the dietary <u>choices</u> available to keep <u>themselves</u> healthy and strong. A horse's genetics know what the horse needs and when. For example – when a horse needs a liver cleansing the brain will send him after thistle. When he needs vitamin E it might send him searching for a blackberry. Etc. If he's eaten quite enough of high-sugar grasses, the hypothesis is he'll switch to the low sugar grasses to balance. When humans attempt to perform these functions, it's usually pure guesswork, and usually late, behind the curve.

I sat on the porch and pondered these for a while. Clearly the more the domestic horse could live and eat like his wild counterpart the healthier and happier he would be. We had a pretty good start at this in California with our "Paddock Paradise" arrangement. They were never confined, were out 24/7 with the herd, and getting plenty of movement, defined by placing their hay in more than 100 small piles all the way around their 1½ acre hillside pasture. (See our Paddock Paradise video on Vimeo & The Soul of a Horse Channel on YouTube). Not what you would typically call a pasture. There was no grass. Just dirt and rock... and dust!

But had we been able to add grass it would've been a microcosm of how horses live in the wild.

Or would it?

At the time, I didn't know how or what horses eat in the wild. I assumed that grass was grass. Off to Google, landing on safergrass.org and a study of *What Feral Horses Eat* by Kathryn Watts.

Ahhh. Now we're getting somewhere.

Her study and several others found on the internet were pretty much the same, varying only by geographical availability. The conclusions were that wild horses eat mostly (80% or better) native and naturalized grasses of various species plus orbs (flowering plants and weeds), shrubs of various kinds, tree leaves and bark, and more. In other words, they have lots and lots of choices and they use them. Ms. Watts found that all the grasses in the wild contained lower sugars than any cultivated pasture grasses she's tested. And *some* of the wild grasses contain *substantially* less sugar than domestic pasture grasses. Thus the hypothesis that the wild horse will balance his own sugar by eating both kinds of grass, along with those orbs, shrubs, tree leaves, etc.

She also points out, as does Pete Ramey, that grasses in the wild tend to be "bunchy" or "patchy", not in thick, tightly-woven carpets like so many domestic pastures. So the horse in the wild has to move more, cover more ground, to get the same amount of forage that a domestic pastured horse is getting. The wild horse is getting less grass per acre, thus less sugar per acre. And more movement which helps digestion and circulation. Plus he's balancing his intake by what his body is telling him he needs. And he has a wide range of choices of forages to accomplish this as he goes about his day.

I was beginning to carve away at the answer. Only it was obviously not *one* "answer," but a whole bunch of answers.

We all want this to be simple, but like so much of life, it just isn't. There is not one *big* difference between the domestic pasture and the wild horse meadow that can solve the sugar problem. There are a *lot* of differences, and each one is important.

Yet the bottom line is simple. Replicate the wild horse lifestyle and diet as closely as your situation permits and you will likely be good to go. And your horse will thank you.

After digging into this for a while now I think I've found "the bugs on the leaves," or rather they have become self-evident, and there are a bunch of them.

Ready?

Here we go:

First, most grassy domestic horse pastures are:

1. Only a single species of grass and nothing else. No orbs, or shrubs, or weeds, or trees. Nada. One choice for the horse. Eat it or go hungry.

2. That single species of grass is usually a "cool season" grass like orchard or timothy because they grow longer into the cooler seasons. Cool season grasses are much higher in sugar content than "warm season" grasses because the cool season grasses contain fructan. Fructan that can continue to build forever as long as there's sun for photosynthesis. Warm season grass contains no fructan, only starch. Starch that is self-limiting because once the organ that holds it is full, production stops. Kathryn Watts has found cool season grasses to have NSC (sugar) percentages as high as 25+%. Warm season grasses are much, much less. The generally accepted NSC maximum as a percentage of a horse's overall diet should be 10% or less.

3. That same single species of grass is usually a genetically modified species to make it heartier and grow longer into the cool sea-

sons. Kathryn Watts' studies find that genetically modified and "improved" grasses are consistently higher in sugar than any natural or unmodified species.

4. The single species of grass in a domestic pasture is usually heavily fertilized with chemical fertilizer (to make it even richer, and thicker). Chemical fertilizer contains large amounts of potassium which in times of stress can be feeding the horse levels of potassium a thousand times the amount he should be getting. This can cause all kinds of internal problems.

5. The single species of grass in a domestic pasture is also probably sprayed with herbicides to kill everything except the grass (plants and weeds that might be giving the horses some of the choices he needs). Note: Chemical poison of any kind, regardless of manufacturers' claims, is not good for the delicate balance of the inner workings of the horse's gut.

6. The single species of grass is also probably sprayed with pesticides from time to time. Another poison.

7. And, lastly, the soil itself can be worn down and depleted of needed nutrients etc when planted and replanted with only the same seed every year, and fertilized and re-fertilized exactly the same year after year.

So I suppose if you're looking for one big issue to hang your hat on, it would be the issue of choice for the horse.

Lots of choices.

Not just one species of highly fertilized cool season grass. But rather many species of grasses, favoring low sugar warm season grasses like Bermuda, and lots of other stuff. All scatter-planted in patches and bunches. Not wall-to-wall. I cannot emphasize enough that if your horse has the choices he needs he will make the right choices to balance his diet and thus himself.

4
UGLY PASTURES

The perfect natural pasture for the horse will be ugly. Big time ugly. It will look uncared for. Not a nice, beautiful, thick carpet of a single species spreading out for acres.

Below are two of Ginger Kathrens' photos of the wild horse meadow atop one of the Pryor Mountains of Montana where Cloud's band and many other wild horses hang out during the Spring and Summer. They head up as soon as the snow melts and don't go down until they're forced to by the onslaught of winter weather. From a distance it looks for the world like any cultivated rich green pasture, but it's not even close. The horses have tons of choices to balance their own diets and apparently handle it all quite well.

Not your pristine, manicured pastoral scene you would expect to see driving through Kentucky, or even our little slice of middle Tennessee. As I said, wild horse pastures are ugly with a capital "U" but are just what the horse needs.

The following shots are a few looks at our hillside pasture, up close and personal. It's hard to discern in these small photos, but each one contains at least some Bermuda, orchard, fescue, Dallis Grass, crab grass, and various orbs and un-named weeds.

As I wrote this in October, our herd's favorite delicacy was that flat seed of a weed that is covered in something like Velcro which sticks to anything that gets within yards of it. The horses were coming in with dozens of those awful things clumped in their forelocks, all over their faces, on their legs, everywhere! As I pulled these pesky seeds off, the horses usually wanted to eat them out of my hand. Obviously there's something there they need or want. If a horse is getting plenty of what he needs or wants, he simply will not eat something that's bad for him. But if he's hungry and something bad is the only choice he has he will eat it.

How many acres per horse? The only answer I know is: *it depends*. We're at approximately 2.75 acres per horse. Last fall, when we arrived, just after we had bush hogged maybe a third of it that had been allowed to grow wild with virtually no grass, and before we had sewn any seed, I was worried that the pasture wouldn't be large enough. But after sewing a bit of orchard and a lot of Bermuda the next spring and summer, there was still plenty of grass in October. I think we're going to be fine. For cutting we follow Melanie Bowles' philosophy at the Horses of Proud Spirit Sanctuary. Nothing ever shorter than 4", grass never longer than 12".

Our two pastures are both open to all the horses at all times. When we moved in, neither pasture had been fertilized for at least eight years. Of course I didn't have sense enough to ask that question before we bought the property, but for reasons I have never fully understood, once again God was taking care of us. The population was mostly weeds when we arrived but we found that once it had been bush hogged there was quite a bit of fescue, crab grass, and other kinds underneath just begging for sunlight. You might recall that rain wasn't an issue that first Fall. We planted maybe 50 pounds of Orchard at the tail end of the season. It was already too late for warm season Bermuda but I didn't know about the difference in sugar levels at that time anyway.

By Spring I was armed with research and when we started sewing the mix was heavily skewed toward Bermuda. Maybe a third of it was orchard grass. And now all of it seems to be doing very well.

We continued to feed one bale of Bermuda hay a day during the hot season, split between morning and night, scattered over a long path through the western pasture to help enforce movement and to help skew diversity toward warm season grasses as we attempted to build our "wild horse meadow". The spring-fed pond is located on the far eastern end of the east pasture, which helps a lot with movement. It's their only water source.

So there it is. That's what we've learned and what we're doing. The logic of it all, as with so much of this journey, has left me wondering why in the world I didn't see it before. But in any case, our horses are the beneficiaries. To change a "traditional" pasture to a "wild" pasture, I suspect, wouldn't be as difficult or take as long as one might think. And it's a whole lot easier to manage a messy pasture than to keep a pasture pristine. Stop all chemicals. Throw out (by hand) a lot of differing seeds trying to favor warm season grass or at least 50/50 with cool season grasses. Hike into the nearest woods and bring back some weeds, seeds of weeds, and brambles, and shrubs. Take the fences off your trees. And manage the pasture only by cutting. Grass does well with cutting, weeds do not. So if you cut with Melanie's plan the weeds will not take over. They'll just be a presence. Or so I've been told, and it seems to be working for us.

And please remember, the object of all this is to be able to leave your horses out, living like horses, around the clock, 24/7, without worry about the amount of sugar your horse might be taking in. Or what that sugar might be doing to the health of your horses. To be able to let the horses monitor and manage their own diet and lifestyle instead of us micro managing their entire life. This is not to say that certain supplements might not be needed to cover deficiencies, which requires testing the grasses, perhaps the soil, observing the horses, and filling in the holes. But definitely cut out all processed feeds, all feeds with grain (sugar), and, of course, all sweet feeds. If you need added weight consider maybe a tiny bit of alfalfa, or rice cold processed bran (we use rice bran). Our herd gets a small forage feed (Triple Crown Safe Starch) morning and night with a bit of rice bran (different for each horse) and a few supplements top dressed, which I believe will be tapered off over time. But that is yet another topic. This one was all about what you can do to a sugar-unfriendly pasture to give your horses the lifestyle and health they were genetically designed to live, the lifestyle they deserve. This September (2014) will mark five full years of our herd being out 24/7 with only the barn breezeway and side shed for occasional shelter, at their choice, not ours. Both are open on both ends so no one can get trapped.

For your horse's sake, please put the bugs back on the leaves.

5
FIVE YEARS AND COUNTING

As this is written we are only a couple of months from the five-year anniversary of our southern California herd's arrival in middle Tennessee, moving from the photo above to the one below.

Quite a difference. Driven home by record-setting mostly wet or mostly dry weather. We were worried sick about their feet which were accustomed to the kind of terrain that horses are genetically designed to live on, like the Great Plains and Great Basin where they evolved for millions of years. Hard and rocky. Not unlike their southern California home. So feet were our number one concern. Especially when we discovered we were moving into the wettest fall on record in middle Tennessee and our horses would not even see dry ground for months, never mind hard and rocky. This would be followed by the worst winter in 25 years, the floodingest spring ever, the hottest summer on record, and the records are still falling as I write this.

And, of course, there were the "Founder Valley" warnings. But we were determined to trust ourselves to figure it out. Determined that our herd would continue to live as natural a lifestyle as possible.

Our herd of six-now-eight were virtually maintaining their own feet in California. Dani Lloyd trimmed every 8-9 weeks, usually doing little more than light maintenance. But they were moving 8-9 miles a day on the kind of terrain pictured above. The trimming schedule changed in middle Tennessee.

Mark Taylor is now trimming every six weeks and the hoof walls are always a bit long by trim day (except in winter). We find ways to ensure a lot of movement every day but the terrain just doesn't provide the wear and tear that they are genetically designed to get. Yet, because it takes 5,000 to 10,000 years to even begin to change the base genetics of any species, Mother Nature has no way of knowing our guys are not on Great Basin-like terrain. She is still growing that hoof as if they were. So we have to help them along with the trim, with movement, and with quite a bit of pea gravel in their well-traveled areas like the barn breezeway, the round pen, and around the pond where they drink.

But with all this, even three to four weeks after a trim, our 32 hooves look for the world like they looked when forged on the southern California high-desert type of terrain.

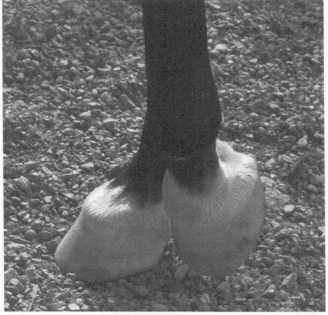

As mentioned before, the feet were my big concern with the move to Tennessee. But the feet turned out to be the least of our worries.

Cash's Left Front Hoof in Tennessee

Cash's Right Front in Tennessee

Several things popped up that our high-desert herd had never experienced before. Not the least of which was that Kathleen's and my "human-nes" always gets in the way. Like how difficult it is sometimes to stay on the horse's end of the lead rope. To think about things from the horse's perspective. Whether it relates to training or lifestyle.

I'll never forget standing out in the rain one cold October day in California, soaked from head to foot because the rain wasn't expected. The temperature was only in the mid-fifties, but to me, sopping wet, that was freezing.

I looked at our horses, heads down, dripping with water, and I just couldn't stand it. I went for the halters and lead ropes and brought them into three covered stalls. The stalls were open, actually only half-covered, with one solid side facing the usual weather assault, but if we'd had a cozy barn with central heating and warm fuzzy pillows I'm sure I wouldn't have hesitated to take them right in. Or cover them with blankets had there been any available.

It's difficult for humans, especially when cold and wet, to understand that the horses do *not* feel like we do. Or eat like we do. Or react like we do. Or live like we do. We want to believe that the horse will always be better with human intervention. Human "help." How can they possibly make it without us?

Later that month I was wandering through a barn in northern Idaho. As I walked down the center aisle, I was struck by how clean it was. Pristine! When the owner happened by I said, "Do you never use this barn? It's so clean."

"Oh sure," he said. "We use it for hay storage."

"What about the horses?"

"They like to be outside."

"Even in the winter? In the snow?"

"Yep."

We were only twelve miles from the Canadian border. Winters are not warm here. I was amazed.

The owner walked around the barn to show me a lean-to he had built which was attached to the side of the structure. Just a roof, with divided but open stalls, to keep the horses separated when eating their supplements. They had free access to this shed, but never came into it except for the feed. Again, I was amazed. This ran so counter to everything I felt for my horses. We want to think of them as children, or big dogs, and treat them in the same manner.

They aren't children, or big dogs.

Not even close.

What sometimes seems too simple for me to grasp is the fact that horses have been around for all those millions of years, evolving to survive as a prey species, and those evolved genetics are precisely the same for every horse on the planet, wild or domestic. Given the opportunity they can take care of themselves. They're built to do it. If not, we would have never heard of the horse. They would've been extinct eons ago.

At both our former California home and the new one in middle Tennessee we have worked hard to mimic the wild horse lifestyle as closely as possible. But it never fails. Just when I think I've *got* it, when I'm certain I understand the concept…WHAP!

Along comes a blow to test my faith.

Last September Mariah quite suddenly went dead lame in her right front foot. With a pounding digital pulse. Couldn't put any weight on it al all. An abscess! Apparently a bad one.

Fear rushed in and faith went right out the window.

It *could've* happened a few days earlier, *before* Kathleen and the twins returned to California to dig in for their last high school year. But it didn't. No, it had to be while I was home alone. With no one to help, or soothe, or listen. I was frozen in place.

Freaked out.

Tharn!

I love that word from *Watership Down*. It's rabbit-speak, and there is simply no English equivalent. It's what happens when a rabbit gets caught in the headlights and is so suddenly petrified that he can neither move nor think.

I was tharn. Our vast experience with horses – almost 5 years at that point – had never shown us an abscess. I was told gory stories of digging out all this gross-looking stuff with a knife and soaking the horse's hoof several times a day. High doses of antibiotics. And all the terrible things that can happen if it's not properly cared for. I was so tempted to violate my firm beliefs, my faith in Mariah's systems and the wild horse lifestyle, and lock her up because she was obviously in a great deal of pain trying to walk and keep up with the herd. But keep up she did, wherever they went. It was painful to watch. I was told the vet should come and dig it out.

At someone's advice I tried soaking her foot in Epsom salts. But she quickly grew tired and annoyed with keeping her foot in a tub for fifteen minutes at a time and finally she said *enough!*

And: *Where's my herd?!*

Determined, she found them, and with each step seemingly excruciating, she followed them off to the grove (she's last in the photo above). Deep down I of course knew that movement meant blood circulation and circulation meant healing but it was buried too deep for me to find and take comfort in at the moment. *But re-*

member this please: stalling a horse with such a condition is exactly the wrong thing to do.

Mariah followed the herd all the way to the grove on the far end of the western pasture (above), between a quarter of a mile and half a mile away from the group photo above. Here she is surrounded by the herd, all just out of frame. With a long walk back to the barn.

I had to quit watching her move. It hurt *me* too much.

"Get a soaking boot. You have to soak," someone said.

I made several phone calls and went out and bought a soaking boot.

It was never used.

When I arrived back at the house with the boot, there was an email waiting from Yvonne Welz, the amazing editor of *The Horses Hoof* magazine. She said: *Joe, when a horse has healthy hooves, abscesses are often here today and gone tomorrow! Just not a big deal. Yes, when the hoof has good blood circulation and lots of movement, the body just absorbs the problem area. Why do abscesses happen in healthy horses? Some sort of trauma or environmental cause, usually.*

Natalie Cruz of Shoe Free Performance Horses went a step further: *The vets won't like this but abscesses will heal themselves. The best thing you can do for your horse is give it a couple of tablets of bute a day for a week or so and baby the horse a bit for your own peace of mind. Keep the horse turned out so it can move which increases blood flow so the abscess either blows out or disintegrates inside the hoof. But check to make sure the horse was not kicked or otherwise injured, of course. If not, and the horse is suddenly dead lame on one hoof, it is usually an abscess. Take a couple of aspirin for your own headache and wait it out. But don't allow anyone to dig it out! This is counterproductive to healing and can actually introduce bacteria into the hoof and cause problems! No need to wrap the hoof either. It just annoys the horse and doesn't help its healing one iota. So drink a glass of wine and prop your own foot up instead. :) Some drawing products like Epsoms salt may help a little bit though I don't use any of them.*

I had barely finished reading these when suddenly Mariah was better. Limping, but putting weight on the hoof. The next morning she was walking fine. A day later she was cantering down our steep hill with the herd racing to the barn for breakfast.

A few months ago we had watched an abscess on Skeeter's belly (caused by an allergic reaction) slowly disappear as the body dissolved it. Likewise my tharnness began to dissolve away leaving an embarrassed logic. Of course, it's the blood circulation that does the dissolving. So why shouldn't Mariah's body do it's job. She has terrific circulation in her feet because she wears no shoes. She gets tons of movement which increases circulation even more. Her diet is good. And her body is working as it's designed to work.

The verse *Oh ye of little faith* came to mind.

Unfortunately appropriate.

The lesson? Nobody says it better than Rick Lamb: *Give them as natural a life as possible. Then get out of the way.*

Anybody want to buy fifteen pounds of Epson Salt?

Throughout the first two years allergy problems from fauna the California herd had never seen before were probably been the biggest issues. More so the first year, so the immune systems are getting a handle on it all. Cash had a ligament pull from sliding down the hill in the snow. There have been a few pricks from thorny brambles allowed to grow too tall. All adding to the learning experience. But although the feet were my biggest concern when we headed to Tennessee, and although we've been through almost five full years of record-setting weather, our herd's feet have been terrific.

We were handed yet another lesson the second Spring because like so many humans hung up with human concepts we brought the herd through the winter at their normal weight, upping rice bran portions to be sure they didn't get too "skinny and unhealthy". The problem with that contorted logic is that horses in the wild will naturally thin down as winter wears on. And they evolved to do so because, of course, the forage is more sparse in the winter, but also they can handle those "rich Spring grasses" much better when they burst into Spring nice and lean.

We didn't see this issue the first Spring because they had been here only about six months and were apparently still adjusting to the move. But this their second year, when the Spring grasses began to emerge – cool season higher sugar grasses always emerge before the warm season grasses containing less sugar – the horses all blimped up pretty good. We missed it in the beginning because we are with them every day so I'm really thankful that Mark Taylor, our hoof specialist, was coming every six weeks. He spotted the extra weight immediately and we slowly but methodically cut way back on the rice bran (which is the only weight maintenance supplement they receive).

Now we let them go into winter with a decent weight but in January we'll start cutting back on the rice bran – watching and judging as we go – so they'll hit the Spring grass season lean and mean so to speak and thereby able to handle the higher sugars with less effort. Just like in the wild.

So here we are marking the five-year anniversary of our guys and gals being out 24/7 on the "rich grasses of middle Tennessee." They're a happy healthy bunch and Kathleen and I are mighty proud parents. As we stress in all of our books, please don't take someone else's word for how you should be caring for your horses just because that's the way it's always been done. Do the research yourself, dig out the answers, and don't stop asking questions until the answers begin to make sense.

Discovering the mysteries of the horse will be a never-ending journey, but the rewards are an elixir. Nothing can make you feel better than doing something good for another being. Not cars. Not houses. Not facelifts. Not blue ribbons or trophies. And there is nothing more important in life than love. Not money. Not status. Not winning. This is the synthesis of our books and why each one came into being.

There are many who teach relationship, riding, and training with principles of natural horsemanship. Others support the benefits of going barefoot with the wild horse trim. Still others write that your horse should eat from the ground, and live without clothes and coverings. Some promote day and night turnout, where your horses can move around continuously. I've found none who advocate the essentials of a wild horse meadow in their pastures. And few have explored how dramatically one without the other can affect the horse and his well-being. Few have put it all together into a single philosophy, a unified voice, a complete lifestyle change for the domesticated horse. When I gave Cash the choice of choice and he chose to trust me he left me with no alternative. No longer could it be what I wanted, but rather what he needed. What fifty-two million years of genetics demanded for his long, healthy, and happy life.

So here we are. Eight happy, healthy horses, all very well adjusted and loving their natural life... as we continue to receive our life lessons from each and every one. We are replenished daily, hourly, by scenes like the ones above and below. On a recent evening Kathleen and I sat on the porch with a glass of wine watching the herd, and talking. "I know in my heart that the philosophy is correct," she said. "That our horses are living the life they should be living, and because of that they should be able to take care of themselves." She paused for a moment, then added, "But it surely feels good to see four and a half years come to an end and be able to witness the hard cold proof of it all." I smiled, teared up a bit, and said simply, "Thank you God."

From our front porch

Follow Joe & Kathleen's Journey

From no horses and no clue to stumbling through mistakes, fear, fascination and frustration on a collision course with the ultimate discovery that something was very wrong in the world of horses.

Read the National Best Seller

The Soul of a Horse
Life Lessons from the Herd

...and the highly acclaimed best selling sequel...

Born Wild
The Soul of a Horse

Go to: www.thesoulofahorse.com

The above links and all of the links that follow are live links in the eBook editions available at Amazon Kindle, Barnes & Noble Nook, and Apple iBooks

WHAT READERS AND CRITICS ARE SAYING ABOUT JOE CAMP

"Joe Camp is a master storyteller." *THE NEW YORK TIMES*

"Joe Camp is a gifted storyteller and the results are magical. Joe entertains, educates and empowers, baring his own soul while articulating keystone principles of a modern revolution in horsemanship." *RICK LAMB, AUTHOR AND TV/RADIO HOST "THE HORSE SHOW"*

"This book is fantastic. It has given me shivers, made me laugh and cry, and I just can't seem to put it down!" *CHERYL PANNIER, WHO RADIO AM 1040 DES MOINES*

"One cannot help but be touched by Camp's love and sympathy for animals and by his eloquence on the subject." *MICHAEL KORDA, THE WASHINGTON POST*

"Joe Camp is a natural when it comes to understanding how animals tick and a genius at telling us their story. His books are must-reads for those who love animals of any species." *MONTY ROBERTS, AUTHOR OF NEW YORK TIMES BEST-SELLER THE MAN WHO LISTENS TO HORSES*

"The tightly written, simply designed, and powerfully drawn chapters often read like short stories that flow from the heart. Camp has become something of a master at telling us what can be learned from animals, in this case specifically horses, without making us realize we have been educated, and, that is, perhaps, the mark of a real teacher." *JACK L. KENNEDY, THE JOPLIN INDEPENDENT*

"This book is absolutely fabulous! An amazing, amazing book. You're going to love it." *JANET PARSHALL'S AMERICA*

"Joe speaks a clear and simple truth that grabs hold of your heart." *YVONNE WELZ, EDITOR, THE HORSE'S HOOF MAGAZINE*

"I wish you could *hear* my excitement for Joe Camp's new book. It is unique, powerful, needed." *DR. MARTY BECKER, BEST-SELLING AUTHOR OF SEVERAL CHICKEN SOUP FOR THE SOUL BOOKS AND POPULAR VETERINARY CONTRIBUTOR TO ABC'S GOOD MORNING AMERICA*

"I got my book yesterday and hold Joe Camp responsible for my bloodshot eyes. I couldn't put it down and morning came early!!! Joe transports me into his words. I feel like I am right there sharing his experiences. And his love for not just horses, but all of God's critters pours out from every page." *RUTH SWANDER – READER*

"I love this book! It is so hard to put it down, but I also don't want to read it too fast. I don't want it to end! Every person who loves an animal must have this book. I can't wait for the next one !!!!!!!!!" *NINA BLACK REID – READER*

"I LOVED the book! I had it read in 2 days. I had to make myself put it down. Joe and Kathleen have brought so much light to how horses should be treated and cared for. Again, thank you!" *ANITA LARGE - READER*

"LOVE the new book… reading it was such an emotional journey. Joe Camp is a gifted writer." *MARYKAY THUL LONGACRE - READER*

"I was actually really sad, when I got to the last page, because I was looking forward to picking it up every night." SABINE REYNOSO - READER

"*The Soul of a Horse Blogged* is insightful, enlightening, emotionally charged, hilarious, packed with wonderfully candid photography, and is masterfully woven by a consummate storyteller. Wonderful reading!" HARRY H. MACDONALD - READER

"I simply love the way Joe Camp writes. He stirs my soul. This is a must read book for everyone." *DEBBIE K - READER*

"This book swept me away. From the first to last page I felt transported! It's clever, witty, inspiring and a very fast read. I was sad when I finished it because I wanted to read more!" *DEBBIE CHARTRAND – READER*

"This book is an amazing, touching insight into Joe and Kathleen's personal journey that has an even more intimate feel than Joe's first best seller." *KATHERINE BOWEN – READER*

Also by Joe Camp

The National Best Seller
The Soul of a Horse
Life Lessons from the Herd

The Highly Acclaimed Best Selling Sequel
Born Wild
The Soul of a Horse

Horses & Stress
Eliminating the Root Cause of Most Health, Hoof & Behavior Problems

Why Relationship First Works
Why and How It Changes Everything

Beginning Ground Work
Everything We've Learned About Relationship and Leadership

Training with Treats
*With Relationship and Basic Training Locked In Treats Can Be
an Excellent Way to Enhance Good Communication*

God Only Knows
Can You Trust Him with the Secret?

Why Our Horses Are Barefoot
*Everything We've Learned About the
Health and Happiness of the Hoof*

The Soul of a Horse Blogged
The Journey Continues

Horses Without Grass
*How We Kept Six Horses Moving and Eating Happily
Healthily on an Acre and a Half of Rocks and Dirt*

Who Needs Hollywood
The Amazing Story of How Benji Became the #3 Movie of the Year

Dog On It
Everything You Need To Know About Life Is Right There At Your Feet

RESOURCES

There are, I'm certain, many programs and people who subscribe to these philosophies and are very good at what they do but are not listed in these resources. That's because we haven't experienced them, and we will only recommend to you programs that we believe, from our own personal experience, to be good for the horse and well worth the time and money.

Monty Roberts and Join up:
http://www.montyroberts.com- Please start here! Or at Monty's Equus Online University which is terrific and probably the best Equine learning value out there on the internet (Watch the Join-Up lesson <u>and</u> the Special Event lesson. Inspiring!). This is where you get the re-lationship right with your horse. Where you learn to give him the choice of whether or not to trust you. Where everything changes when he does. Please, do this. Learn Monty's Join-Up method, either from his Online University, his books, or DVDs. Watching his *Join-Up* DVD was probably our single most pivotal ex-perience in our very short journey with horses. Even if you've owned your horse forever, go back to the begin-ning and execute a Join Up with your horse or horses. You'll find that when you unconditionally offer choice to your horse and he chooses you, everything changes.

You become a member of the herd, and your horse's leader, and with that goes responsibility on his part as well as yours. Even if you don't own horses, it is absolutely fascinating to watch Monty put a saddle and a rider on a completely unbroken horse in less than thirty minutes (unedited!). We've also watched and used Monty's *Dually Training Halter* DVD and his *Load-Up trailering* DVD. And we loved his books: *The Man Who Listens to Horses, The Horses in My Life, From My Hands to Yours, and Shy Boy.* Monty is a very impressive man who cares a great deal for horses.

http://www.imagineahorse.com- This is Allen Pogue and Suzanne De Laurentis' site. I cannot recommend strongly enough that everyone who leaves this eBook Nugget ready to take the next step with treats and vocabulary should visit this site and start collecting Allen's DVDs (he also sells big red circus balls). Because of his liberty work with multiple horses Allen has sort of been cast as a trick trainer, but he's so much more than that. It's all about relationship and foundation. We are dumbfounded by how Allen's horses treat him and try for him. His work with newborn foals and young horses is so logical and powerful that you should study it even if you never intend to own a horse. Allen says, "With my young horses, by the time they are three years old they are so mentally mature that saddling and riding is absolutely undramatic." He has taken Dr. Robert M.

Miller's book *Imprint Training of the Newborn Foal* to a new and exponential level.

Frederick Pignon – This man is amazing and has taken relationship and bond with his horses to an astounding new level. Go to this link: (**http://www.youtube.com/watch?v=w1YO3j-Zh3g**) and watch the video of his show with three beautiful black Lusitano stallions, all at liberty. This show would border on the miraculous if they were all geldings, but they're not. They're stallions. Most of us will never achieve the level of bond Frederick has achieved with his horses but it's inspiring to know that it's possible, and to see what the horse-human relationship is capable of becoming. Frederick believes in true partnership with his horses, he believes in making every training session fun not work, he encourages the horses to offer their ideas, and he uses treats. When Kathleen read his book *Gallop to Freedom* her response to me was simply, "Can we just move in with them?"

<u>**Natural Horsemanship**</u>: This is the current buzz word for those who train horses or teach humans the training of horses without any use of fear, cruelty, threats, aggression, or pain. The philosophy is growing like wildfire, and why shouldn't it? If you can accomplish everything you could ever hope for with your horse and still have a terrific relationship with him or her, and be re-

spected as a leader, not feared as a dominant predator, why wouldn't you? As with any broadly based general philosophy, there are many differing schools of thought on what is important and what isn't, what works well and what doesn't. Which of these works best for you, I believe, depends a great deal on how you learn, and how much reinforcement and structure you need. In our beginnings, we more or less shuffled together Monty Roberts (above) and the next two whose websites are listed below, favoring one source for this and another for that. But beginning with Monty's Join-Up. Often, this gave us an opportunity to see how different programs handle the same topic, which enriches insight. But, ultimately, they all end up at the same place: When you have a good relationship with your horse that began with choice, when you are respected as your horse's leader, when you truly care for your horse, then, before too long, you will be able to figure out for yourself the best communication to evoke any particular objective. These programs, as written, or taped on DVD, merely give you a structured format to follow that will take you to that goal.

> http://www.parelli.com- Pat and Linda Parelli have turned their teaching methods into a fully accredited college curriculum. We have four of their home DVD courses: *Level 1, Level 2, Level 3,* and *Liberty & Horse Behavior.* We recommend them all, but especially the first three. Of-

ten, they do run on, dragging out points much longer than perhaps necessary, but we've found, particularly in the early days, that knowledge gained through such saturation always bubbles up to present itself at the most opportune moments. In other words, it's good. Soak it up. It'll pay dividends later. Linda is a good instructor, especially in the first three programs, and Pat is one of the most amazing horsemen I've ever seen. His antics are inspirational for me. Not that I will ever duplicate any of them, but knowing that it's possible is very affirming. And watching him with a newborn foal is just fantastic. The difficulty for us with *Liberty & Horse Behavior* (besides its price) is on disk 5 whereon Linda consumes almost three hours to load an inconsistent horse into a trailer. Her belief is that the horse should *not* be *made* to do anything, he should *discover* it on his own. I believe there's another option. As Monty Roberts teaches, there is a big difference between *making* a horse do something and *leading* him through it, showing him that it's okay, that his trust in you is valid. Once you have joined up with him, and he trusts you, he is willing to take chances for you because of that trust, so long as you don't abuse the trust. On Monty's trailer-loading DVD Monty takes about one-tenth the time, and the horse (who was impossible to load before Monty) winds up loading himself from thirty feet away, happily, even playfully. And his trust in Monty has progressed as well, because he reached beyond his comfort zone and learned it was okay. His trust was confirmed. One thing the Parelli program stresses, in a way, is a followup to Monty Roberts' Join-Up: you should spend a lot of time just hanging out with your horse. In the stall, in the pasture, wherever. Quality time, so to speak. No agenda, just hanging out. Very much a relationship enhancer. And don't ever stomp straight over to your horse and slap on a halter. Wait. Let your horse come to you. It's that choice thing again, and Monty or Pat and Linda Parelli can teach you how it works.

http://www.chrislombard.com/ - An amazing horseman and wonderful teacher. His DVD *Beginning with the Horse* puts relationship, leadership and trust into simple easy-to-understand terms.

http://www.downunderhorsemanship.com- This is Clinton Anderson's site. Whereas the Parellis are very philosophically oriented, Clinton gets down to business with lots of detail and repetition. What exactly do I do to get my horse to back up? From the ground and from the saddle, he shows you precisely, over and over again. And when you're in the arena or round pen and forget whether he used his left hand or right hand, or whether his finger was pointing up or down, it's very easy to go straightaway to the answer on his DVDs. His programs are very task-oriented, and, again, there are a bunch of them. We have consumed his *Gaining Respect and Control on the Ground, Series I through III* and *Riding with Confidence, Series I through III.* All are multiple DVD sets, so there has been a lot of viewing and reviewing. For the most part, his tasks and the Parellis are much the same, though usually approached very differently. Both have served a purpose for us. We also loved his *No Worries Tying DVD* for use with his Australian Tie Ring, which truly eliminates pull-back problems in minutes! And on this one he demonstrates terrific desensitizing techniques. Clinton is the only two-time winner of the Road to the Horse competition, in which three top natural-horsemanship clinicians are given unbroken horses and a mere three hours to be riding and performing specified tasks. Those DVDs are terrific! And Clinton's Australian accent is also fun to listen to… mate.

The three programs above have built our natural horsemanship foundation, and we are in their debt. The following are a few others you should probably check out, each featuring a highly respected clinician, and all well known for their care and concern for horses.

http://www.robertmmiller.com - Dr. Robert M. Miller is an equine veterinarian and world renowned speaker and author on horse behavior and natural horsemanship. I think his name comes up more often in these circles than anyone else's. His first book, *Imprint Training of the Newborn Foal* is now a bible of the horse world. He's not really a trainer, per se, but a phenomenal resource on horse behavior. He will show you the route to "the bond." You must visit his website.

Taking Your Horse Barefoot: Taking your horses barefoot involves more than just pulling shoes. The new breed of natural hoof care practitioners have studied and rely completely on what they call the wild horse trim, which replicates the trim that horses give to themselves in the wild through natural wear. The more the domesticated horse is out and about, moving constantly, the less trimming he or she will need. The more stall-bound the horse, the more trimming will be needed in order to keep the hooves healthy and in shape. Every horse is a candidate to live as nature intended. The object is to maintain their hooves as if they were in the wild, and that requires some study. Not a lot, but definitely some. I now consider myself capable of keeping my horses' hooves in shape. I don't do their regular trim, but I do perform interim touch-ups. The myth that domesticated horses *must* wear shoes has been proven to be pure hogwash. The fact that shoes degenerate the health of the hoof and the entire horse has not only been proven, but is also recognized even by those who nail shoes on horses. Successful high performance barefootedness with the wild horse trim can be accomplished for virtually every horse on the planet, and the process has even been proven to be a healing procedure for horses with laminitis and founder. On this subject, I beg you not to wait. Dive into the material below and give your horse a longer, healthier, happier life.

http://www.hoofrehab.com/– This is Pete Ramey's website. If you read only one book on this entire subject, read Pete's *Making Natural Hoof Care Work for You.* Or better yet, get his DVD series *Under the Horse,* which is fourteen-plus hours of terrific research, trimming, and information. He is my hero! He has had so much experience with making horses better. He cares so much about every horse that he helps. And all of this comes out in his writing and DVD series. If you've ever doubted the fact that horses do not need metal shoes and are in fact better off without them, please go to Pete's website. He will convince you otherwise. Then use his teachings to guide your horses' venture into barefootedness. He is never afraid or embarrassed to change his opinion on something as he learns more from his experiences. Pete's writings have also appeared in *Horse & Rider* and are on his website. He has taken all of Clinton Anderson's horses barefoot.

The following are other websites that contain good information regarding the barefoot subject:

http://www.TheHorsesHoof.com– this website and magazine of Yvonne and James Welz is devoted entirely to barefoot horses around the world and is surely the single largest resource for owners, trimmers, case histories, and virtually everything you would ever want to know about barefoot horses. With years and years of barefoot experience, Yvonne is an amazing resource. She can compare intelligently this method vs that and help you to understand all there is to know. And James is a super barefoot trimmer.

http://www.wholehorsetrim.com - This is the website of Eddie Drabek, another one of my heroes. Eddie is a wonderful trimmer in Houston, Texas, and an articulate and inspirational educator and spokesman for getting metal shoes off horses. Read everything he has written, including the pieces on all the horses whose lives he has saved by taking them barefoot.

Our current hoof specialist in Tennessee is Mark Taylor who works in Tennessee, Arkansas, Alabama, and Mississippi 662-224-4158 http://www.barefoothorsetrimming.com/

http://www.aanhcp.net- This is the website for the American Association of Natural Hoof Care Practioners.

Also see: **the video of Joe: Why Are Our Horses Barefoot? On** The Soul of a Horse Channel on YouTube.

Natural Boarding: Once your horses are barefoot, please begin to figure out how to keep them out around the clock, day and night, moving constantly, or at least having that option. It's really not as difficult as you might imagine, even if you only have access to a small piece of property. Every step your horse takes makes his hooves and his body healthier, his immune system better. And it really is not that difficult or expensive to figure it out. Much cheaper than barns and stalls.

> **Paddock Paradise: A Guide to Natural Horse Boarding** This book by Jaime Jackson begins with a study of horses in the wild, then describes many plans for getting your horses out 24/7, in replication of the wild. The designs are all very specific, but by reading the entire book you begin to deduce what's really important and what's not so important, and why. We didn't follow any of his plans, but we have one pasture that's probably an acre and a half and two much smaller ones (photos on our website www.thesoulofahorse.com). All of them function very well when combined with random food placement. They keep our horses on the move, as they would be in the wild. The big one is very inexpensively electrically-fenced. *Paddock Paradise* is available, as are all of Jaime's books, at **http://www.paddockparadise.com/**

Also see the video **The Soul of a Horse Paddock Paradise: What We Did, How We Did It, and Why** on The Soul of a Horse Channel on YouTube.

New resources are regularly updated on Kathleen's and my: **www.theSoulofaHorse.com** or our blog **http://thesoulofahorse.com/blog**

Liberated Horsemanship at:
http://www.liberatedhorsemanship.com/
Scroll down to the fifth Article in the column on the right entitled Barefoot Police Horses

An article about the Houston Mounted Patrol on our website: Houston Patrol Article

The following are links to videos on various subjects, all found on our The Soul of a Horse Channel on YouTube:

Video of Joe: Why Are Our Horses Barefoot?

Video of Joe: Why Our Horses Eat from the Ground

Video: Finding The Soul of a Horse

Video of Joe and Cash: Relationship First!

Video: The Soul of a Horse Paddock Paradise: What We Did, How We Did It, and Why

Don't Ask for Patience – God Will Give You a Horse

The next 2 links are to very short videos of a horse's hoof hitting the ground. One is a shod hoof, one is barefoot. Watch the vibrations roll up the leg from the shod hoof... then imagine that happening every time any shod hoof hits the ground: to view go to The Soul of a Horse Channel on YouTube:

Video: Shod Hoof
Video: Barefoot Hoof

Find a recommended trimmer in your area:

http://www.aanhcp.net

http://www.americanhoofassociation.org

http://www.pacifichoofcare.org

http://www.liberatedhorsemanship.com/

Valuable Links on Diet and Nutrition:

Dr. Juliette Getty's website:
http://gettyequinenutrition.biz/

Dr. Getty's favorite feed/forage testing facility:
Equi-Analytical Labs:
http://www.equi-analytical.com

For more about pretty much anything in this book
please visit one of these websites:

www.thesoulofahorse.com

http://thesoulofahorse.com/blog

www.14handspress.com

www.thesoulofahorseblogged.com

The Soul of a Horse Fan Page on Facebook

The Soul of a Horse Channel on YouTube

Joe and The Soul of a Horse on Twitter
@Joe_Camp

Made in the USA
San Bernardino, CA
03 March 2015